The Story of the Political Reformers of 1793-4

A neighbourhood history by Wally Macfarlane

The Scottish Martyrs

"When our ashes shall be scattered by the winds of Heaven the impartial voice of future time will rejudge your verdict". So spoke Thomas Muir at his trial in August 1793 in Edinburgh when he was found guilty of Sedition and sentenced to be transported for 14 years to Botany Bay, thus becoming the first of the group of political reformers known to history as the Scottish Martyrs.

It is many years now since my friend, Tom Gibson, aroused my interest when he asked me what I knew about the Scottish Political Monument in Nunhead Cemetery. As Rye Hill, where I live, backs on the Water Board which adjoins the cemetery in Linden grove, once called Cemetery Road, there was a compulsion to go and see for myself this link between my country and my adopted parish. It is no reflection on the Scots that they do not know their own history. It was a rather blank area, certainly in my time, in the school curriculum. Bury its history and you bury a nation.

The Nunhead Monument is of solid granite, 33 feet high and weighing 40 tons. Sited at the confluence of two gravel walks near the entrance the obelisk commands much attention with inscriptions on each of its five sides. The monument was erected in February 1851 and the quotation from the address to the Jury by Joseph Gerrrald, a fitting epilogue to their story, has defied the weathering of the elements as no doubt the founders intended it should. Probably the first portrait of the Monument is that reproduced in the Illustrated London News of 26th Nov. 1853, a copy of which is retained in Southwark Council's Local History Library. The main citation reads:-

"To the memory of Thomas Muir, Thomas Fysche Palmer, Joseph Gerrald, William Skirving and Maurice Margarot. Sentenced to transportation for advocating with fearless energy the principle of Parliamentary Reform."

How did it happen?

Towards the end of the 18th Century the demand for political change was rife. British radicalism was stirred by the American War of Independence in 1775 and the French Revolution of 1789. Both events were spanned by Thomas Paine, inventor, bridge-builder and radical pamphleteer. Paine had emigrated to America on the eve of the struggle of the Colonists. His

"Common Sense", of which the theme was Independance, was commended by George Washington as having "Worked a powerful change in the minds of many men". Back in England twelve years later and still building bridges Paine wrote his "Rights of Man" in which he demolished the argument of Edmund Burke that the Settlement of 1688 had established the British Constitution "For Ever". "Man's rights", wrote Paine, "pertain from the time he is born until the time he is laid in the grave. He has no rights over the unborn. He has no rights over the dead". This blast at the hereditary platform in the wake of the French Revolution won for Paine a summons to appear at the Bar but, sensibly, he neglected to appear. Trials not of a felony could take place in the absence of the accused and, although defended by the eminent Thomas Erskine, Paine was found guilty and sentenced to 'Outlawry'.

Societies for the propagation of Parliamentary Reform sprouted all over the country, Paine's tracts being in great demand. The mass of the people had no vote and with few exceptions only men of landed property could sit in Parliament. Pocket-boroughs with few inhabitants had the right to elect Members of Parliament while well-populated areas had no representation at all. The most notorious was Old Sarum with two M.P.s representing seven inhabitants. When the "Friends of the People" was formed in Glasgow, Thomas Muir was one of the first to join. He had entered Glasgow University at the age of twelve and was intended for the Kirk but had fallen foul of the authorities, who recommended that Muir, and ten others, be not admitted to classes, an indication that students have not changed so much after all. Muir switched to Law, and graduated M.A. before moving to Edinburgh where he concluded his studies and was admitted a Member of the Faculty of Advocates. In 1792 he emerged as one of the leading figures of the "Friends of the People" Society.

However, if Parliamentary Reform was in the air, the Prime Minister, William Pitt the Younger, was determined to crush it. With the Republican movement raising its ugly plebeian head abroad the Government was determined to prevent it from spreading; all manifestations of support for Parliamentary Reform were branded as seditious. Henry Dundas, the Home Secretary, had an army of informers covering every meeting of the dissidents and when he had decided to make an example of a prominent reformer, Thomas Muir was the selected victim. So it was that Robert Dundas, Lord Advocate of Scotland and nephew of the Home Secretary, was himself the prosecutor in what became one of the most ruthless, biased and venomous trials of the century.

THOMAS MUIR

Should fate command me to the farthest verge
Of the green earth, to distant barbarous climes:
————'tis nought to me: —— I cannot go
Where UNIVERSAL LOVE not smiles around—
From seeming evil still educing good,
And better thence again, and better still,
In infinite progression.-——

Thomas Muir

Muir was arrested on 2nd January 1793, charged with sedition and lodged in Tolbooth. Released on bail he made the mistake of visiting France where he sought to convey the opinion of the Scottish Reformers that the threatened execution of the French monarch would do harm to the Reform Movement. During Muir's stay Louis XVI was executed and with England declaring war on the new republic the French ports were sealed up. Muir made a delayed journey home via Ireland and was arrested in Stranraar as an outlaw. Although offered the legal assistance of the famous Erskine, Muir decided to conduct his own defence.

Muir defended himself with great spirit. "What has been my crime?", he asked. "Not the lending to a relative of mine a copy of Mr Paine's book, not the giving away a few copies of an innocent and constitutional publication, but for having dared to be, according to the measure of my feeble abilities, a strenuous and active advocate for an equal representation, in the House of the People." He ended his plea, "Gentlemen of the jury, this is perhaps the last time that I shall address my country. I have explored the tenor of my past life. Nothing shall tear from me the record of my former days. The enemies of Reform have scrutinised, in a manner unexampled in Scotland, every action I have performed, every word I have uttered. Of crimes most foul and horrible have I been accused. Of attempting to rear the standard of civil war, to plunge this land in blood and to cover it with desolation. "My crime is for having dared to be an advocate of Reform. It is a good cause - it shall ultimately prevail - it shall finally triumph."

Lord Braxfield, in his summing up addressed the jury thus:- "Two things the Jury must attend to which require no proof. First, that the British Constitution is the best that ever was since the creation of the world and it is not possible to make it better. Yet Mr Muir has gone among the ignorant country folk making them forget their work and told them that a Reform was absolutely necessary for preserving their liberty, which, if it were not for him, they would never have thought to be in danger." This jewel from the Judge was no less than an extra speech for the prosecution. The verdict of Guilty occasioned no surprise but the sentence of 14 years transportation left everyone, including the jury, thunderstruck.

Laments were loud throughout the country at the harsh sentence and this and the others which followed must have been in the mind of Robert Burns, Scotland's national bard, when in September of that year he wrote to Mr George Thompson and enclosed his freshly written "Scots Wha Hae", remarking that he had been roused into writing it by "the recollection of that glorious struggle for Liberty associated with the glowing ideas of other struggles *not quite so ancient.*"

Thomas Fysche Palmer

Public Enemy No 2 was the Reverend Thomas Fysche Palmer. Palmer was a native of Bedfordshire and was educated at Eton. He took a Bachelor of Divinity after securing a B.A. and a M.A. but later became dissatisfied with Church of England doctrine and moved to Montrose in Scotland where he espoused Unitarianism. He was a compulsive writer and wrote many theological tracts. He became an eloquent advocate of Universal Suffrage and was charged with writing a seditious tract which he then distributed. The tract was in fact written by a George Mealmaker, himself a witness at the trial.

The story of Palmer's case and his defence is told in Howell's State Trials. The offending pamphlet had been distributed by William Skirving and two Dundee booksellers had taken a number for sale. It contained anti-war sentiments and prophesied economic ruin for the people who, without Universal Suffrage, were powerless to stay the course of events. Palmer's counsel made a powerful defence based upon the Liberty of the Press and speeches made in Parliament by supporters of Universal Suffrage against whom there was no suggestion of charges for sedition being made. The judge accepted that Palmer might not have been the author of the "Seditious" tract but he was responsible for its publication. He was sentenced to seven years transportation.

Despite the sentences on Muir and Palmer, "The Friends of the People" went ahead with plans for a Convention in Edinburgh, and delegates from 45 Scottish Societies and three Societies from England were elected. William Skirving was the Secretary of the Convention and Joseph Gerrald and Maurice Margarot were delegates from the London Corresponding Society. The Convention was dispersed by the authorities and Skirving, Gerrald and Margarot were arrested.

LKAY 1793

The Rev.d

T. F. PALMER.

Edinburgh published as the Act directs by W. Skirving

I. KAY fecit 1794

CITIZEN SKIRVING

Secretary to the British Convention
A Tried Patriot and an Honest Man.

William Skirving

Skirving was the son of a prosperous farmer and was educated for the Kirk. Nevertheless it was farming he turned to and according to Frank Clune, the Australian writer, he was a candidate for the Chair of Agriculture in the University of Edinburgh. Braxfield was again the chairman of the panel of judges, all of whom were peers of the realm. Skirving was charged with circulating seditious handbills, of making seditious speeches and of seeking to have a meeting after the Convention had been dispersed. Although the terms Convention and Delegate were common usage in Scotland the prosecution sought to give them a French connotation. Skirving had no counsel and defended himself.

Braxfield, when addressing the Jury, cunningly invited them to see sedition in a time of war as high treason and asserted "That only the greatest union of the nation could be supported in the bloody war against the most profligate monsters that ever disgraced humanity".

Skirving replied with dignity. "Conscious of my innocence and that I am not guilty of the crimes laid to my charge, this sentence can only affect me as the sentence of man. It is long since I laid aside the fear of man as my rule. I shall never walk by it.... I know that what has been done here will be rejudged. That is my comfort and all my hope".

Said the London Morning Post of 17th January 1794: "Mr Skirving, who was lately sentenced to fourteen years transportation in Scotland, leaves a wife and eight helpless children behind him".

Maurice Margarot

Maurice Margarot, as his name suggests, was of French stock, his father being in the wine trade. Margarot senior was a known supporter of John Wilkes in the mid-century trials so there was a radical tradition in the family. At his trial Margarot showed himself to be something of a showman and a very verbose character indeed. He tantalised the Court with his non-stop discourse; in fact he talked too much for his own good. He laid into his accusers "Rather imprudently," say some historians, and certainly without effect. Knowing how the Court had dealt with Muir, Palmer and Skirving in no way intimidated Margarot, however, who proceeded to indict Judge Braxfield as being manifestly biased and therefore unfit to make judgement. When at last Braxfield got a word in it was to sentence Margarot to fourteen years in Botany Bay.

MAURICE MARGAROT.

Questions put to the Lord Justice Clerke.

Marg: Did you use these words — What sho.ᵈ you think of giving
him 100 lashes together with Botany Bay — or words to that purpose.

Lᵈ J.Clk: Go on   put your quest.ⁿ if you have any more.

Marg: Did any person — Did a Lady say to you that the Mob
would not allow you to whip him. — my Lord did you
not say that the Mob would be the better for letting a
little *BLOOD*.

Published as the Act directs Feb.y 1795 by H.D.Symonds N.º P.

9

Joseph Gerrald

Joseph Gerrald appeared in the dock on January 3rd 1794. By that time his colleagues were already assembled at the ports awaiting sail. When arrested, Gerrald had been granted bail and he returned to London. Although he was beseeched by his friends to get away across the Channel he elected to return to Edinburgh and stand trial. He was not a well man although only 30 years of age when arrested.

Gerrald was born in the West Indies where his Irish father had property and was sent to a private school in Stanmore to be educated. He returned home, married and practised at the Bar in Pennsylvania. He later came to London again in 1787 and became active in the agitation for Parliamentary Reform. He was tried on 3rd March 1794 and made a spirited defence. He objected in Court to Lord Braxfield trying him on the grounds that he had prejudged his claim to impartiality when he announced publicly that he would make the prisoners squeal. He challenged the charge that to seek Reform was seditious and he challenged the selection of the Jury all of whom had come from the Association of Goldsmiths. "Gentlement", he said "If fugitivity is in the eye of the law deemed to be a presumption of guilt, appearance, by parity of reason, must be deemed to be a presumption of innocence."

Sir Walter Scott spoke of "Gerrald's unrivalled oratory". An unsolicited compliment came from Braxfield himself when, in his summing-up, he said, "I look upon this man as a very dangerous member of Society for he has eloquence enough to persuade the people to rise in arms". Braxfield showed his crudeness when Gerrald referred to Christ as one of the very great men who had themselves been Reformers, by chuckling audibly "And muckle ye mak o' that, He was hanget". The trial lasted four days yet the hand-picked Jury returned inside 20 minutes with a verdict of Guilty. Although Gerrald was clearly a sick man and unfit for a long sea-voyage he was also sentenced to 14 years transportation to Botany Bay.

The State trials of the "Scottish Martyrs", as they had become known, engendered nation-wide feeling. On a wet day in April 10,000 people gathered in Sheffield "To determine the propriety of addressing the King on behalf of the persecuted patriots, citzens Muir, Palmer, Skirving, Margarot and Gerrald and to petition the House of Commons for a Reform in the Representation of the People." In Parliament pleas were made for a reversal of the savage sentences. Throngs of well-clad gentry posted down to the Hulks to visit the Reformers before they sailed for Van Diemen's Land.

OMNE SOLUM FORTI PATRIA.

I.KAY 1794

JOSEPH GERRALD

A Delegate to the British Convention.

THE TRIAL AND ACQUITTAL OF THOMAS HARDY

There is little doubt but that the wide-spread protest of public-spirited men and women paved the way for the acquittal of Thomas Hardy when he was tried in London on 24th October 1794. Hardy, a Scot from Larbert in Stirlingshire, was secretary of the London Corresponding Society and he was defended at the Old Bailey trial by that Thomas Erskine who had defended Thomas Paine. For the defence Erskine called upon Richard Sheridan, actor and politician and sometime Member of Parliament. Sheridan vouched that Hardy had visited him at his request to discuss the structure and aims of the Society that Sheridan might better put his case in Parliament for parliamentary reform. There was no secrecy about the aims of the Society.

Another powerful witness for Hardy was Charles Lennox, Duke of Richmond. Lennox was educated at Westminster School and graduated at Leyden University, the finishing school in the Netherlands for European Royalty. He was at odds with his kinsman George III on the American Colonies and also on the Irish question. On 2nd June 1780 Richmond had introduced a Reform Bill in the House of Lords and his proposals became the scripture of every Society promoting the freedom of the franchise. The proposals provided a framework for annual Parliaments, universal suffrage and electoral districts.

Hardy's trial drew large crowds which overflowed into Ludgate Hill, Snow Hill and Smithfield. It was known at 12.30 on the ninth day that the Jury had retired to consider their verdict and when three hours later a roar was heard from the Court House and handkerchiefs waved from a window, there was a tumult of cheering and Hardy's carriage was hauled from the Old Bailey to Piccadilly by his jubliant supporters. During Hardy's sojourn in gaol his house was attacked by a mob of ruffians armed with sticks and stones. His wife, although expecting a baby, escaped through a side window. She was badly bruised. Soon after, she died in labour and the baby was still-born. When Hardy was released he had no home to return to and no family. He survived to live until 1832, the year of the first Reform Bill. The Society which he had helped to form and to which the members had pledged to contribute one penny per week, was finally vindicated.

AT SEA IN THE "SURPRISE"

Although it might have been assumed that the group banished to Botany Bay would be blood-brothers for life, such was not the case. When the "Surprise" arrived on 25th October 1794 after its seven month voyage the Captain reported to the Governor of the Colony that Palmer and Skirving had plotted to cause the crew to mutiny, but that he had foiled them and put them in irons. A counter charge made by Palmer and Skirving claiming false arrest, injury to their person and expressing their "Astonishment, indignation and horror" is contained in the Historical Records of New South Wales. There is little doubt but that the "Plot" was a fiction. The plot was "leaked" to the Captain by a rival group of convicts and it is likely that the Reformers' contention that their sentence did not include "Servitude" was unpopular with the other convicts and proved to be an irritant to them. Arising from out of what his colleagues called his collusion with the Captain, on the voyage, Margarot was expelled from their Society by his colleagues. As he had prevailed upon the authorities to allow his wife to share his exile Margarot was not entirely alone.

The four men - Gerrald arrived later - are recorded as having refused to be included on the ration strength of the Colony. At that time the strength was 3,211 persons of whom there were 546 women convicts under forty, 1,362 male convicts, 310 soldiers many of whom were paying the price for unsoldierly behaviour on American battlefields, the wives and children of the officers and officials and a number of free settlers. Today it is a great honour to be a descendant of a member of the "First Fleet" which founded the colony on 26th January 1788 and included six convict transports. The Governor of the Colony was fair but firm with the Reformers and they were apportioned houses "Contagious" to each other.

When Joseph Gerrald arrived at Sydney on the 5th November 1795 he had undergone 14 months imprisonment and seven months on board the transport "Sovereign" on its 13,000 mile voyage. He was already in a declining state of health and died on 6th March 1796. Palmer said of Gerrald's grave "He was buried in a garden forming part of a little plot which he purchased at Farm Cove. The inscription on his tomb records that he died a martyr to the liberties of his country in the 35th year of his age."

I have searched Farm Cove, now one of the most beautiful Botanic Gardens in the world, for a plaque or commemorative stone in memory of Gerrald but without success.

Within three days of Gerrald's death William Skirving died of a dysentery not uncommon in the Colony. Governor Hunter in a dispatch which is quoted by Frank Clune wrote thus:- "Mr William Skirving, a very decent, quiet and industrious man, who had purchased a farm already cleared and was indefatigable in his attention to its improvements, was seized with a violent dysentery just as the labour of the harvest was over and died on the 9th of the same month. Therefore there are of five persons sent out under that particular charge, only two, Mr Palmer and Mr Margarot, who live quiet and retired."

In "The Memoirs and Trials of the Scottish Martyrs" a copy of which is in the British Museum, there is a reference to a letter from Skirving to his wife written on the "Surprise" which gives poignancy to his trust in the Deity: "My increasing love for you constrains me already to begin writing to you. My unshaken faith in God our Saviour that He is and will continue to be the husband of my widow and the Father of my fatherless, while the designs of His providence require the continuation of our separation, continues to be my support in this unpleasant voyage".

In a letter describing the last days of Gerrald and Skirving, Palmer wrote "In the month of February Mr Muir made his escape in the 'Otter'. He is to visit the Friendly Isles, the Phillipines and China and thence back to Boston, America, a voyage of two years. He went in excellent health and spirits as his constitution is made of iron. With Margarot I have no intercourse so that I am left alone with none to associate with but my friends Ellis and Mr Boston." Ellis resided with Palmer in Dundee and elected to share his banishment. Mr Boston and his wife sailed in the "Surprise" as free settlers.

Muir had an adventurous voyage. On arrival at the Friendly Isles he and an officer from the ship found themselves being escorted by natives to visit the chief in the village with little or no option. A display by the chief of captured heads indicated that it was time to depart and they quickly made their way back to the ship with some resentment being shown by the natives. When the "Otter" arrived at Nootka Sound Muir was advised of two British warships in the area. Vancouver Island was then a source of contention between Britain and Spain although a treaty had been drawn up at Nootka in 1792. Muir decided to make for Mexico and transferred at short notice to a Spanish ship bound for Monterey. Although he was received with great kindness by the Spanish Governor, Muir's request for a Passport to proceed to Washington was referred to the Viceroy at Vera Cruz. Muir took advantage of his long stay to write home to his parents and to many friends in Scotland. These letters were intercepted by the Viceroy and are now in the archives in Seville. The Viceroy must have thought that a meeting of Muir with George Washington would not help the Spanish cause and he arranged for Muir to be sent to Spain.

Muir sailed on the Spanish ship "Ninfa" which, with the "St. Elena", was pursued near Trafalgar by the British 74-gun "Irresistible" and the 36-gun frigate "Emerald". In the fighting Muir was wounded but escaped to shore when the "Ninfa" was captured. He was taken to a Spanish hospital. Muir was badly disfigured and lost an eye. Despite this he was eventually able to leave for France where he received a hero's welcome and was fêted in Bordeaux and in Paris. Paris was then a haven for the dissidents of Europe and Muir met Paine and Wolf Tone with many others. When they met Tone expressed the desire of his group that Muir desist from going into print on the Irish question. Whatever divergence of opinion there was clearly remained unresolved as Tone wrote in his diary; "Of all the vain obstinate blockheads that I ever saw, I never met his equal."

There were two factions in the Irish camp and Muir presumably echoed the views of the rival camp of "Napper Tandy". A few months later Wolf Tone was intercepted by a British Fleet when on his way to lead the Irish Rising of 1798. He died in prison whilst awaiting trial.

In the Guildhall Registry of Britons married abroad I came across the entry a few years ago of Matilda Wolf Tone married at the British Embassy in Paris to Thomas Wilson on 19th August 1816 and witnessed by William Wolf Tone and Edward Wetherington, an indication that the Irish patriot's family found political asylum in the French Republic.

Although Muir had engaged himself in writing his memoirs and had made a request to the French authorities for financial assistance pending their publication, this did not materialise and his situation worsened. Very soon afterward he passed into obscurity and on the 26th January 1799 in his 34th year Thomas Muir succumbed to his wounds and privation and died at Chantilly, a Paris suburb.

We return again to Botany Bay where Palmer proved himself to be a person of some business acumen. He was not averse to buying cheap and selling dear and as this was the stock-in-trade of the military elite who ran the colony and were its quartermasters, Palmer was doing the done thing. From trading with ships entering the harbour he took the logical step of forming a syndicate to trade with his own ship. He ran a service to Norfolk Island but apparently without a licence. One of Palmer's letters home carried a request for a copy of an encyclopedia covering the building of ships. His last letter from Sydney on 10th September 1798 stated that he had sold his 100 acres and planned to sail for New Zealand in the syndicate's ship "The Plumo", originally a Spanish vessel. From New Zealand they sailed to Macao for a load of timber, but ran into difficulties with a leak and put into Guam. One story states that their ship was made a prize of war but that they were treated kindly by the Spanish Governor although his country was at war with Britain. Certain it is that Palmer was stricken with dysentery from which he had never been free since his first voyage in the convict ship. So this dedicated Reformer and theologian breathed his last in the remote island of the Ladrones on what was to be his return-voyage home.

In his many letters Palmer gave an interesting picture of the shape of the New Colony in Sydney and on the character of the natives. Describing how he and Ellis stayed with some natives in order to show them how to hoe and plant the ground "That they might soon be civilised" he reminds us that when Man creates the Means of Subsistence for himself, he takes an evolutionary leap forward. The Australian Aborigine had not reached this stage. Palmer commented too on the absence of chiefs and priests in the Aborigine society, "Despite which, they have a discipline by which every member of the Commonwealth is coerced into good order."

Maurice Margarot was the only Reformer of those who stood trial in Scotland to return home. In contrast with the other political prisoners he was in constant conflict with the authorities. No doubt this could be attributed not only to traits of personality but to his deeply held Republicanism. At one time he was consigned to Tasmania and on another to Newcastle by Governors who wished Margarot from under their feet. He returned to England in 1810, sixteen years after his sentence. In the years which followed he was called upon to give evidence to an "Enquiry into the effects of Transportation" as a mode of punishment." He was one of the few who found the money for his passage home. Maurice Margarot died in Bull Place, St Pancras in the year 1815 in his 66th year.

THE TWO MONUMENTS

It was on 20th February 1837 that at a meeting of notables in the Crown and Anchor, Clerkenwell Green, it was decided to commemorate the Scottish Martyrs by erecting a monument in the two capital cities, Edinburgh and London. Interestingly, the Crown and Anchor is a few doors up on the Green from the building where the Social Democratic Federation published "Justice" and Lenin edited "Iskra". It is now the home of the Marx Memorial Library.

The meeting was chaired by Joseph Hume MP, the member for Montrose, but there is little doubt but that the impetus came from the rising tide of Chartism. We read of what Judge Braxfield had called the Rabble marching in May the following year (1838) to Fleshers Haugh, Glasgow Green, behind 70 banners and forty bands in a demonstration of 300,000 people. The Chartists, heirs of the Political Reformers, were on the march.

So it was that on 24th August 1844 three thousand gathered in the old Calton Burial ground, Edinburgh to see Hume lay the foundation stone of the Scottish Memorial to the Martyrs. As a student, at Edinburgh University, Joseph Hume had witnessed the events of 1793-4. On this occasion 400 members of the Complete Universal Suffrage Association, dressed in black, marched past the Law Courts where the Martyrs had been unjustly sentenced, and thence to the Cemetery. Thomas Muir's agent at the trial, William Moffat and Mr Skirving, son of the Convention's secretary, were present to be acclaimed by the assembly.

In his memorable book "The Scottish Martyrs" Frank Clune concludes thus:- "From my library high over Sydney Cove I view the roadstead where the convict transport "Surprise" dropped anchor. Imprisoned in it were the shackled fighters for liberty, banished from the British Isles, only one of whom was to return home. They were not silenced. They had the courage of their convictions. They died for them."

Frank Clune has passed on and his book is out of print. In the reading rooms of the National Library in Sydney I perused it with other documents which are now part of the Library's collection of "Australiana". Nowhere have I come across any reference to a Commemorative ceremony to mark the unveiling of the Monument to the Scottish Martyrs in London's Nunhead in February 1851. By then the Chartist Movement was already on the wane in the wake of the collapse of the Kennington Petition in 1848.

In the political vacuum which prevailed between Chartism and Labourism there was no beating heart to give to Joseph Hume in 1851 what he and the Parliamentary Radicals had been able to draw upon in 1837. But that in no way diminishes the solid contribution which was his and which, in granite, bears the words of Joseph Gerrald for all to see.

"The experience of all ages should have taught our rulers That persecution can never efface principles. Individuals may perish but truth is eternal."

APPENDIX I

SOUTHWARK April 19, 1792.
At a MEETING held at the THREE TUNS TAVERN,
Mr SAMUEL FAVELL in the Chair,

Refolved,
"That a Society be formed in Southwark for the cultivation and diffufion of Political Knowledge.

Refolved,
"That the Society be denominated "THE FRIENDS OF THE PEOPLE".

Refolved,
That the following be the DECLARATION of this Society.

"Considering that ignorance, forgetfulnefs, or contempt of the RIGHTS OF MEN are the fole caufes of public grievances, and of the corruption of Government; "this Society, formed for the purpofe of inveftigating and afferting thofe Rights, and of uniting their efforts, with thofe of their fellow Citizens, for correcting national abufes, and reftraining exorbitant and unneceffary Taxation, do hereby declare -

1ft. That the great end of civil fociety is GENERAL HAPPINESS.

2nd. That NO FORM OF GOVERNMENT is good, any further than it fecures that object.

3rd. That all Civil and Political Authority is derived from the people.

4th. That equal active Citzenfhip is the unalienable right of all Men; Minors, Criminals, and Insane Perfons excepted.

APPENDIX II

Joseph Gerrald

An Obituary by Thomas Fysche Palmer

Here lies Joseph Gerrald, Barrister of the State of Pensylvania, condemned by the Court of Justiciary in Edinburgh in defiance of the law of the land, to 14 Years transportation beyond the seas for meeting in a Convention of the People as delegates from the popular Societies in Great Britain to obtain a reform in the Commons House of Parliament.

Having suffered many months the rigours of a loathsome prison, tantalised to the last by the Ministry with hopes of liberty, broken in health and emaciated by a consumption caused by the foul air he breathed, although almost unable to walk, he was hurried away in the dead of night and weighted with irons and sent by a flagitious apostate, a condemned felon to Botany Bay.

Gerrald was a man of singular endowment, of deep sagacity, great application and retentive memory. The Grecian and Roman authors were at his tongue's end and he was fluent in French, German and Italian languages. He was deeply versed in metaphysical, moral and political knowledge and as Godwin observed, "From his various information the wisest of us might have been content to learn."

From genius and these other stores, his eloquence was, as his judge exclaimed, irresistible. He could convince the mind of reason by weight of argument and call to his assistance every motion of the heart. "He was too", wrote Godwin, "placable and generous to an extreme". The Magnanimity of his spirit and the purity of his sense of honour could only be understood by those who made them the subject of personal observation.

Torn from the bosom of that polished and learned society of which his gay spirits and acquirements made him the delight and the ornament, most inhumanly sentenced to that of ruffian robbers and the offscourings of mankind, he lingered through two years and died on 16th March 1796, a martyr to the liberties of his country.

Bibliography

The Edinburgh Magazine   Jan 1837   unsigned
Freedom Struggles   T.A. Jackson
Thomas Muir   J. Earnshaw
Historical Records of New South Wales
The Scottish Martyrs   Frank Clune
Historical Records   Southwark Library

Published by Friends of Nunhead Cemetery 1983
Reprinted 1991

Printed by Lindsay Ross International Limited, London & Oxford
Phototypeset by PDR Typesetting Ltd., Leicester

Photographs: British Museum, John Stathatos

Cover illustration: Ron Woollacott

ISBN 0 9508881 0 9